## OVER 70 FUN ACTIVITIES FOR ADULTS!

# Adult Activity Books

## COLORING & PUZZLES

**An Activity Book for Adults
Featuring: Coloring, Sudoku, Word
Search, Mazes, Cryptograms and
more Logic Puzzles**

Thank you for purchasing this adult activity book! It is filled with 70+ relaxing activities to entertain you, reduce stress and challenge your critical thinking skills with activities such as: coloring, mazes, word scrambles, crossword puzzles, word search puzzles and more. There are fun activities for all skill levels in this book from beginners to advanced.  Have fun and enjoy your new activity book!

# Want a freebie?

Check out the end of the book to get a fun FREE gift!

## Look for more Adult Activity Books
## by Mattison Savage

# Want to play FREE games?

**Play FREE video versions of our games here:**

## https://bit.ly/mattisonsavage

**Subscribe to our channel to get notifications of new games!**

# PUZZLE INSTRUCTIONS

## NUMBER BLOCKS

The goal is to try to fill in the missing numbers. The missing numbers are integers between 0 and 9 and the numbers in each row add up to totals on the right side of the grid. The numbers in each column add up to the totals along the bottom of the grid. Also, the diagonal lines add up the totals on the right.

## MATH SQUARES

The goal is to try to fill in the missing numbers. Begin by using the number 1 through 16 to complete the equations. Each row is a math equation and each number is only used once. Complete your work from left to right. Also, each column is a math equation and you will need to complete column equations from top to bottom.

## NONOGRAMS

You have a grid of squares, which must be either filled in black or marked with X. Beside each row of the grid are listed the lengths of the runs of black squares on that row. Above each column are listed the lengths of the runs of black squares in that column. Your goal is to find all of the black squares. Each number indicates the number of black squares on each row and column.

Think logical. Take a look at this example:

If the run starts at the beginning of the row it will end at the second square:

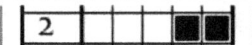

If the run ends at the end of the row it will start from the second square at the end of the row

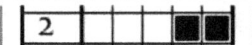

## LETTER TILES

Unscramble the tiles to reveal the message

## FALLEN PHRASES

A fallen phrase puzzle is a puzzle where all the letters have fallen to the bottom, are mixed up but remain in the same row.

The goal is to unscramble the message. First, fill in any blank spaces with just one letter underneath. Next, figure the two word options. Finally, you will have to use trial and error to keep filling in the blanks until you solve the puzzle.

## CRYPTOGRAMS

Cryptograms substitute letters of the alphabet by representing them with another. Start by solving one letter at a time. Then make the best guess. Use your clues and work in pencil to solve the puzzle.

# Find the Pattern

*Solve the puzzle.* **Puzzle A**

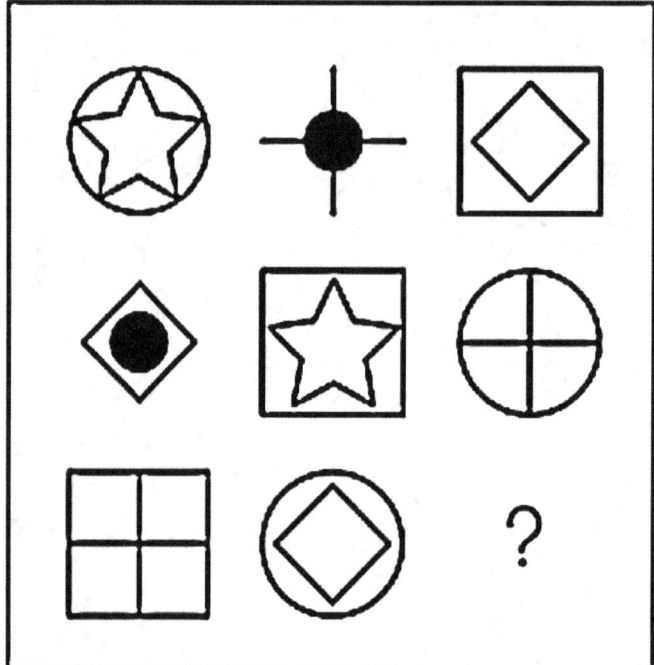

## CHOOSE ANSWER

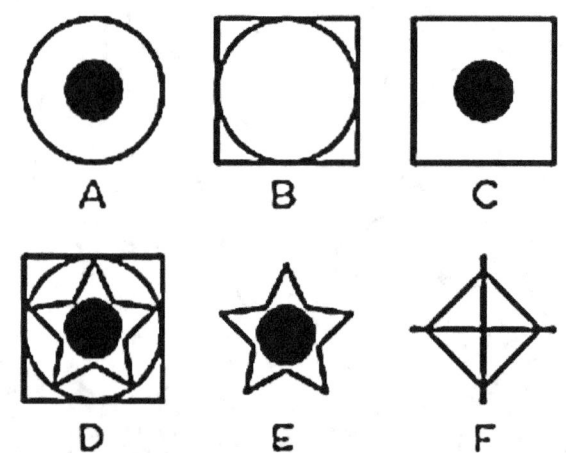

# Word Search 1

*Solve the puzzle*

```
K V F U N D A M E N T A L L A C I S U M
D R W W Z E T Q P C P U U C W E A P O N
O G H L U A O T R E E C L X U P P C N H
C M E E O T G R A E F O L M V C K E M C
U Y I B D O K I S S T O Z G A T H E R I
M L M S E X U A L H W C H R O A D S Y H
E E A P P R O X I M A T E L Y B Y S W W
N R V S C F L N D I N I N G S T L A B H
T D R K U E G B C G N I D D E W R L C X
L E A A G O O E U U O O Q R E O A G E E
V F P A E B R I G B O J O V C S E A E G
O I L I D N N E S D I Y A M D G U R C B
C C U L A S G E G A E C Q D Z Y F B I Q
G I W H T N R Q H N T L E V O B A D D J
E T G A E V O F R I A B W S W O U C B R
K M N O A A I O V Q C D U O D T P B D E
X C E T G G V I S O R R Y E N D Q U R V
E P I H H H S G A L E N A P I K O W C I
Q O S T C T U D O C T O R Y C L C K J R
N M W A X S H T R O W N N I C Q U A N W
```

| | | |
|---|---|---|
| ABOVE | FREE | PIANO |
| ACKNOWLEDGE | FUNDAMENTAL | RELY |
| ACTIVIST | GATHER | RIVER |
| APPROXIMATELY | GLASS | ROAD |
| BOAT | INSTANCE | SCHEME |
| CLOTHING | KISS | SEXUAL |
| DANGEROUS | LEGAL | SORRY |
| DEFICIT | LOUD | WEAPON |
| DINING | MOON | WEDDING |
| DOCTOR | MUSICAL | WHICH |
| DOCUMENT | NEAR | WORTH |
| EARLY | OBSERVATION | |
| FEAR | ODDS | |
| FIGHT | PANEL | |

# Sudoku 1

*Solve the puzzle*

| 7 | 2 | 3 |   |   |   | 1 | 5 | 9 |
|---|---|---|---|---|---|---|---|---|
| 6 |   |   | 3 |   | 2 |   |   | 8 |
| 8 |   |   |   | 1 |   |   |   | 2 |
|   | 7 |   | 6 | 5 | 4 |   | 2 |   |
|   |   | 4 | 2 |   | 7 | 3 |   |   |
|   | 5 |   | 9 | 3 | 1 |   | 4 |   |
| 5 |   |   |   | 7 |   |   |   | 3 |
| 4 |   |   | 1 |   | 3 |   |   | 6 |
| 9 | 3 | 2 |   |   |   | 7 | 1 | 4 |

# Odd One Out 1

*Find the one that is different.*

# Maze 1

*Solve the puzzle*

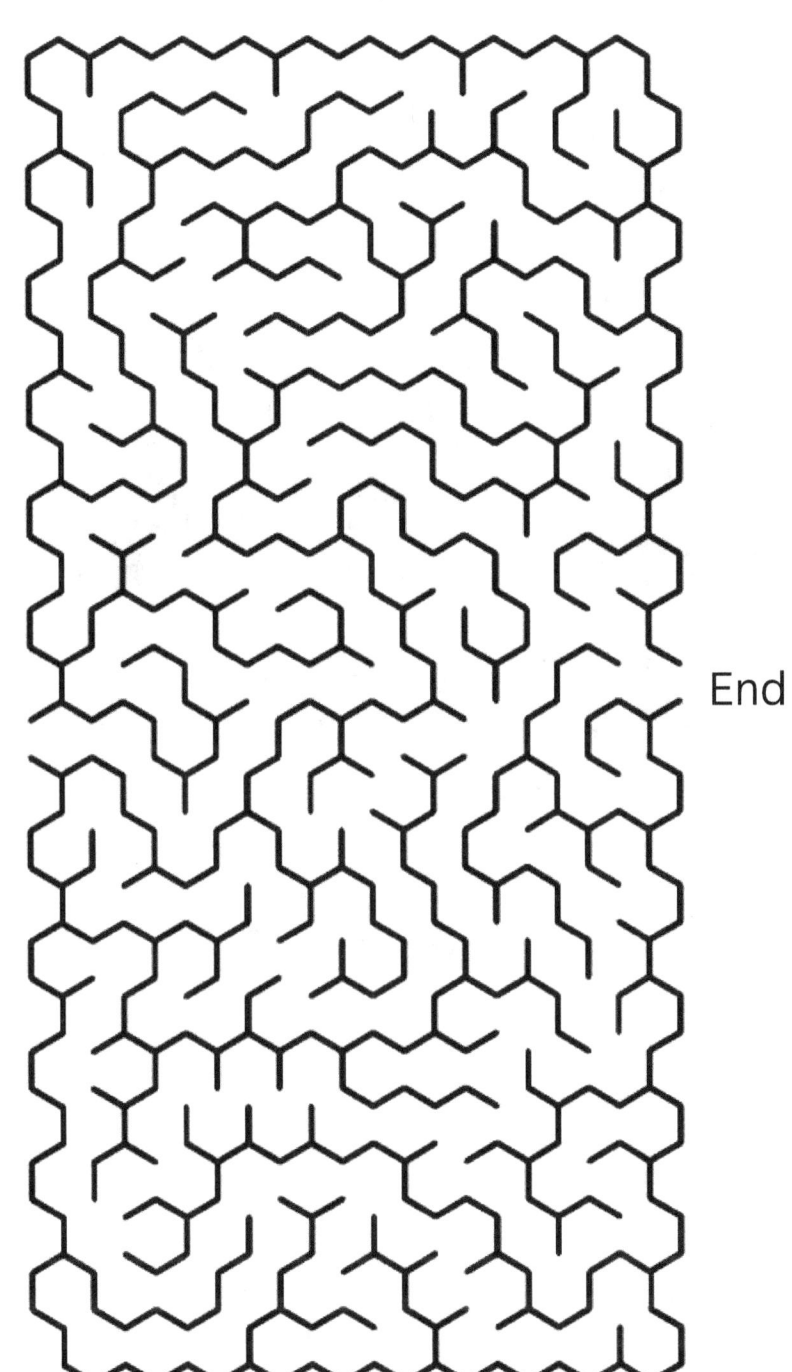

Start

End

# Fallen Phrases 3

*Solve the puzzle.*

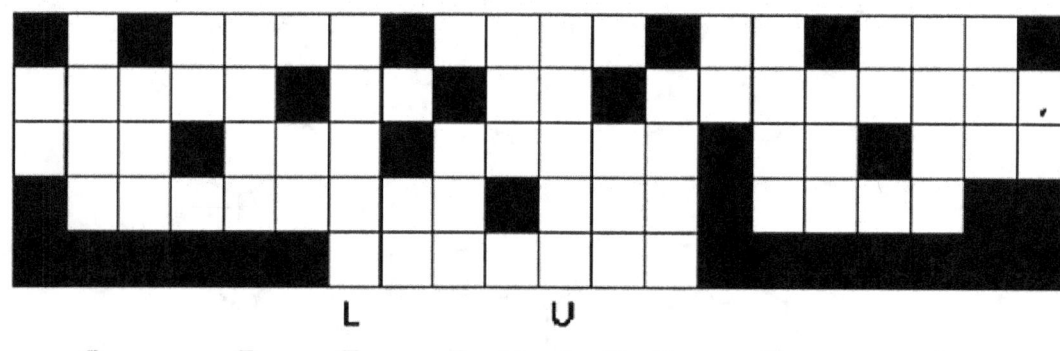

```
                    L           U
     O      E       E     E V A I D     I           A
     I D S T R P R L R A N H     W I I H S
  F I O W T H O U S A F T L I N M T L E
  M P R F E E F T M Y E E N E S L E L L
```

## Puzzle C

# Math Squares

*Solve the puzzle.*

|   | × |   | + |   | / |   | 7 |
|---|---|---|---|---|---|---|---|
| - | ■ | - | ■ | - | ■ | + |   |
|   | - |   | + |   | × |   | 30 |
| × | ■ | - | ■ | / | ■ | + |   |
|   | - |   | / |   | + |   | 10 |
| × | ■ | - | ■ | + | ■ | / |   |
|   | + |   | - |   | + |   | 38 |
| 52 |   | -29 |   | -1 |   | 2 |   |

**Puzzle A**

# Word Puzzles
## *Opposites*
*Write the letter of the correct matching opposite word*

| | | | |
|---|---|---|---|
| 1. | _____ | brave | a. lend |
| 2. | _____ | build | b. up |
| 3. | _____ | bold | c. upwards |
| 4. | _____ | borrow | d. moist |
| 5. | _____ | diseased | e. majority |
| 6. | _____ | down | f. cheerful |
| 7. | _____ | downwards | g. destroy |
| 8. | _____ | dreary | h. cowardly |
| 9. | _____ | dry | i. healthy |
| 10. | _____ | minority | j. accidental |
| 11. | _____ | intentional | k. meek |
| 12. | _____ | humble | l. proud |

# Maze 2

*Solve the puzzle*

Start

End

# Crossword 1

*Solve the puzzle*

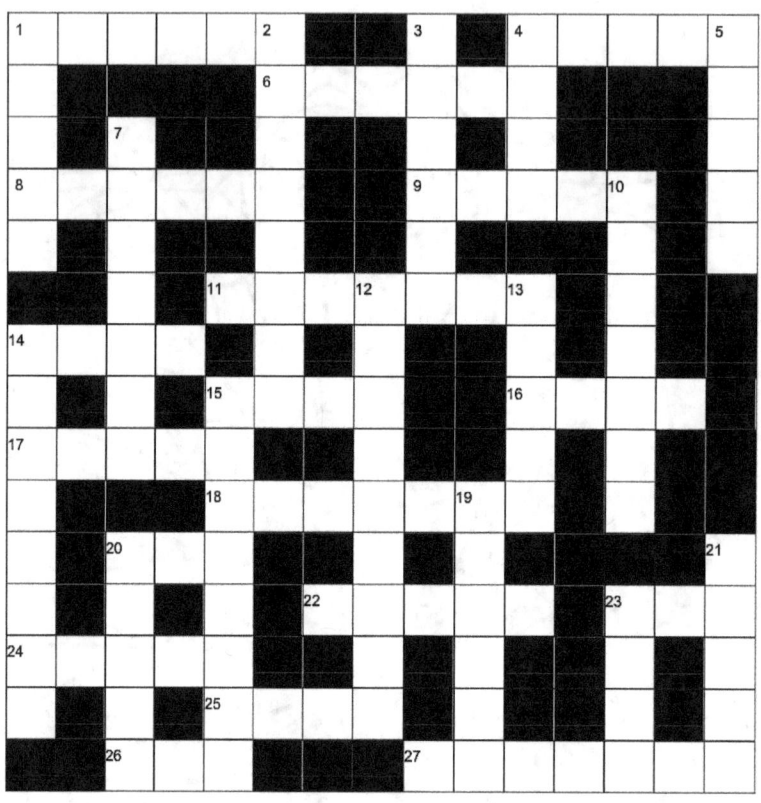

<table>

| <u>Across</u> | |
|---|---|
| 1 | Ark site after the conquest of Canaan (6) |
| 4 | Hopeful lover's plucking (5) |
| 6 | Region in Risk (6) |
| 8 | Makes another proposal (6) |
| 9 | 'To Autumn' poet (5) |
| 11 | Stag's pride (7) |
| 14 | "... what ___ lurks in the hearts of men?" (4) |
| 15 | Reaction from an angry cat (4) |
| 16 | What the connected have (4) |
| 17 | "Don't You Know" songstress (5) |
| 18 | Of the deep-sea floor (7) |
| 20 | Divot's material (3) |
| 22 | Some Finns (5) |
| 23 | Highlander's hat (3) |
| 24 | Reply to "Sez who?" (5) |
| 25 | Agenda, informally (4) |
| 26 | Go below the horizon, (3) |
| 27 | Requirement for e-commerce (7) |

</table>

<table>

| <u>Down</u> | |
|---|---|
| 1 | California missionary founder (5) |
| 2 | 1952 Olympics site (8) |
| 3 | New Jazz star, e.g. (6) |
| 4 | Salt-N-___ ("Shoop" group) (4) |
| 5 | "--- Theme" (music-box favorite) (5) |
| 7 | Outflow (7) |
| 10 | Three-dimensional (7) |
| 12 | Battle of the Alamo, notably (9) |
| 13 | Slender part of the back (5) |
| 14 | Soonest (8) |
| 15 | Car part that helps prevent whiplash (8) |
| 19 | Dream (6) |
| 20 | Economy and medium (5) |
| 21 | Mosey (5) |
| 23 | Dustin's "Tootsie" costar (4) |

</table>

# Number Blocks
## Solve the puzzles.

|     |     |     |     |
|-----|-----|-----|-----|
|     |  8  |     |     |
|     |     |     |     |
|  1  |     |     |     |
|     |  3  |  4  |     |

|     |
|-----|
|  6  |
| 21  |
| 14  |
| 11  |
| 11  |

| 15 | 13 | 12 | 17 |
|----|----|----|----|

| 15 |
|----|

**Puzzle A**

|     |     |     |     |
|-----|-----|-----|-----|
|     |  6  |     |     |
|     |  2  |     |     |
|  7  |     |  3  |  5  |
|  5  |     |     |     |

|     |
|-----|
| 17  |
| 21  |
| 14  |
| 21  |
| 18  |

| 21 | 14 | 21 | 18 |
|----|----|----|----|

| 17 |
|----|

**Puzzle B**

# Letter Tiles

*Solve the puzzle.*

### Puzzle A

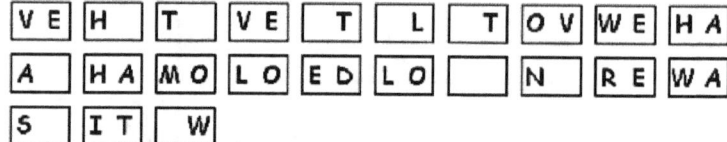

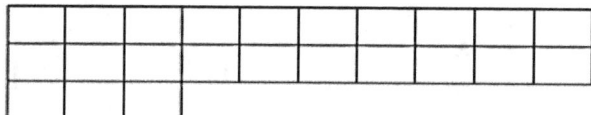

### Puzzle B

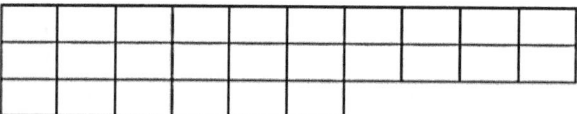

### Puzzle C

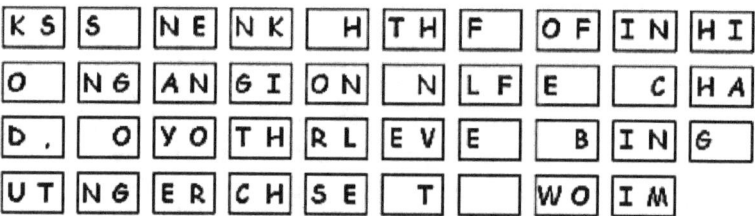

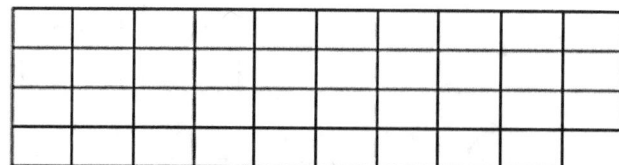

# Sudoku 2

*Solve the puzzle*

| | | 7 | 1 | 5 | | 9 | | |
|---|---|---|---|---|---|---|---|---|
| | | 9 | 4 | 3 | | | | |
| 5 | | | | | 2 | | 1 | 3 |
| | | 6 | 5 | | 4 | | 2 | 9 |
| 4 | 3 | | | 8 | | | 5 | 7 |
| 9 | 7 | | 3 | | 1 | 4 | | |
| 7 | 6 | | 2 | | | | | 5 |
| | | | | 9 | 6 | 2 | | |
| | | 3 | | 4 | 5 | 6 | | |

# Crossword 2

*Solve the puzzle*

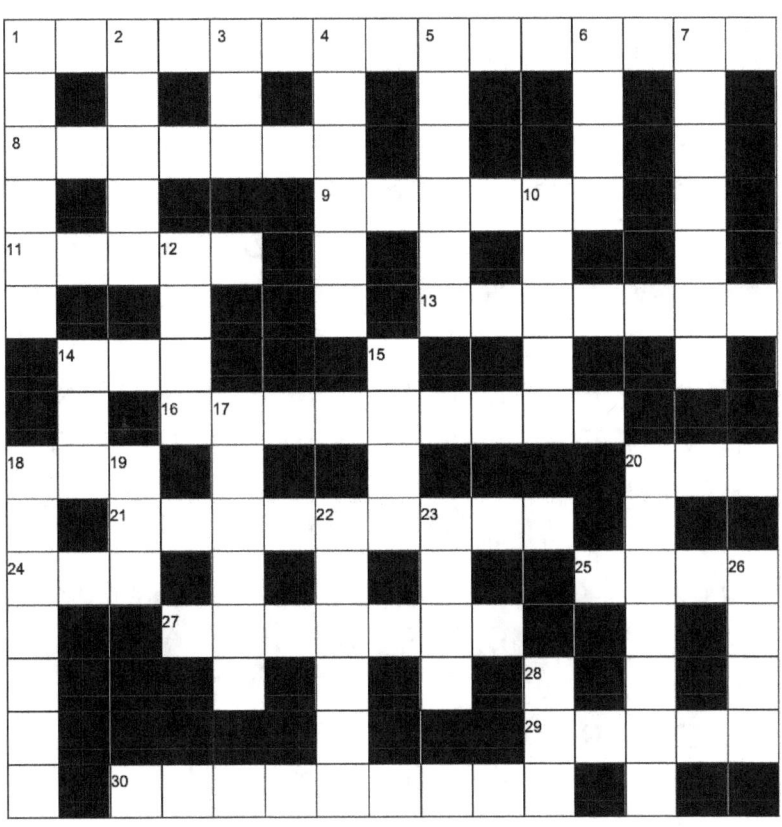

## Across

| | |
|---|---|
| 1 | "Raiders of the Lost Ark" movie genre (15) |
| 8 | Atrocity (7) |
| 9 | Without creating disarray (6) |
| 11 | Motown celebrity (5) |
| 13 | Said of an active person (7) |
| 14 | Chicken-King separator (3) |
| 16 | Communication means at the office (9) |
| 18 | Confident crossword solver's choice (3) |
| 20 | Type of lab (3) |
| 21 | Capone's political position? (9) |
| 24 | Horseplayer's letters (3) |
| 25 | Kesey and Berry (4) |
| 27 | Pharmacists notations (7) |
| 29 | Cake toppers (5) |
| 30 | Actor who said "Only the gentle are ever really strong" (9) |

## Down

| | |
|---|---|
| 1 | ___ santé (French toast) (6) |
| 2 | Duke or dame (5) |
| 3 | 'Is it a boygirl?' (3) |
| 4 | 'Am so!' retort (6) |
| 5 | Shrew (6) |
| 6 | Human-shaped mug (4) |
| 7 | Cast again (7) |
| 10 | Bedfordshire town and airport (5) |
| 12 | Plunder (4) |
| 14 | Curry taken in the morning (3) |
| 15 | Sit-down occasion (4) |
| 17 | Kind of sampling (6) |
| 18 | Like something that's going around? (7) |
| 19 | C.I.A. (3) |
| 20 | What Ben Adhem did (7) |
| 22 | Connects with a memory (6) |
| 23 | "Napoleon" director Gance (4) |
| 26 | Coming and going spots (4) |
| 28 | Grenade activator (3) |

# Word Search 2

*Solve the puzzle*

```
J X I N T E L L E C T U A L C S L L E W
F U B H G Q B N E D I S A P P E A R N F
M B T E B E W C C W M S I N A H C E M R
N W U D L I C C N T C A R T N O C Q E E
E K M J S O M I A V E R O U G H L Y X Q
R I X D W D N H T E N T I R E L Y R P U
K A O N C K K G S O I P R O C E E D E E
X M E V F P W L I W N M E T I V N I N N
J C B G C F U A S M O V I X T U W F S T
T S P I R I T T S E E D U T I T T A E L
O Q R P X M T T A D A K S J K L K V G Y
N E O U T R I A F I R Y U P S Y P N I V
E P M F I W M C T T M Y N F V S I S U M
W R I Q M N B K A O E Q P Z Z W O Z M U
O E N Z D R U P S R D K P R A Q A R T Z
L T E E A L S B Z U V Z Y R E W R Q C Z
L E N T T S E R R A H E D E I U P Y D O
O N T V N G B N X O L A U T I R I P S F
F D H I G H L Y R A N M C A P A B L E B
T O O L Z Q V D Z A H D E C I S I O N X
```

| | | | |
|---|---|---|---|
| ADMIT | DECISION | HIGHLY | SPIRITUAL |
| ARMED | DISAPPEAR | INTELLECTUAL | SUBMIT |
| ARREST | DRAWING | INVITE | TONE |
| ASSISTANCE | EDITOR | MECHANISM | TOOL |
| ATTACK | ENTIRELY | NOTICE | WELL |
| ATTITUDE | EXPENSE | PRETEND | WISDOM |
| BELONG | FAIR | PROCEED | |
| CAPABLE | FOLLOW | PROMINENT | |
| CONTRACT | FREQUENTLY | ROUGHLY | |
| CROSS | GEAR | SPIRIT | |

# Slice Puzzle 2

*Solve the puzzle. Draw each figure in the matching letter and number square below.*

| A1 | B2 | C2 | A4 |
| C3 | D4 | C1 | B1 |
| D2 | A3 | C4 | A2 |
| B3 | D3 | B4 | D1 |

|   | 1 | 2 | 3 | 4 |
|---|---|---|---|---|
| A |   |   |   |   |
| B |   |   |   |   |
| C |   |   |   |   |
| D |   |   |   |   |

# Kakuro 1

*Solve the puzzle. The rules of Kakuro are simple - place the numbers 1 to 9 into the puzzle grid so that each continuous horizontal or vertical run of empty squares adds up to the value to the left of it or above it respectively. This value is shown either to the right or below a diagonal line.*

# Sudoku 3

*Solve the puzzle*

| 1 |   |   |   |   |   |   |   | 9 |
|---|---|---|---|---|---|---|---|---|
|   | 4 |   | 2 | 6 | 1 |   | 3 |   |
|   | 6 |   |   | 5 |   |   | 1 |   |
|   |   | 5 | 6 |   | 3 | 4 |   |   |
| 8 | 1 | 4 | 7 |   | 5 | 3 | 9 | 6 |
|   |   | 9 |   | 1 |   | 7 |   |   |
|   |   |   | 9 | 3 | 4 |   |   |   |
| 4 | 8 |   | 5 | 7 | 2 |   | 6 | 3 |
| 3 |   |   |   |   |   |   |   | 5 |

# Word Search 3

*Solve the puzzle*

```
T O O R N A G N I T T E S V O T E E E A
B Z K C F R S K I A V S P I N E J B C L
Q Z R Z I E G P Y E S Q Y A X R A M N E
A M O N G Y J B X H L E A V E E E U A U
W S T D G W G I J U L D A R C D R I T U
A N V E F A T N E I P A B J J N M B S I
R X E K M L C N F M W U Q B V U D Z M F
M R B A Z B O E F E T S R R Y O V L U I
U U O N R N T R F N T R L E Q F A O C V
S S D A P I M T E E L E N A G R S X R C
I H I P M E M M K T Q P O D G O Q V I I
C N R E H Z E R X N E P L E H P D T C N
A J W T R G A K S A Q L L S I H T S U O
L L L N N M Y H T N I Y H M O N T H H R
X K Q A T M E K O Y T O C T M O D E L T
J F R N W G O C L W Y S J F A W T C P C
Z R D D A C Q H H H N T C O N S I S T E
A P H U K N I H T E L L A C E R C Z J L
Q Y L T N E U Q E R F I O B L F X E X E
K A P Z B B Q O R E R U T C A F U N A M
```

| | | |
|---|---|---|
| AMONG | INNER | PERSUADE |
| ANYWHERE | LARGELY | RECALL |
| ARRANGEMENT | LAWYER | ROOT |
| ATHLETE | LEAVE | RUSH |
| BRAIN | LIFETIME | SETTING |
| BREAD | LOTS | SPIN |
| CIRCUMSTANCE | MANUFACTURER | THEM |
| CONSIST | MARKET | THINK |
| ELECTRONIC | MODEL | THIS |
| FOUNDER | MONTH | VOTE |
| FREQUENTLY | MUSICAL | |
| HEAT | NAKED | |
| HELP | NONE | |

# Crossword 3

*Solve the puzzle*

## Across

| | |
|---|---|
| 1 | Whether to aim at 7 or 10, in bowling? (13) |
| 7 | Biblical movie in the making, in wide screen. (7) |
| 8 | They're too often inflated (4) |
| 9 | ___ one's laurels (6) |
| 12 | Long and narrow (6) |
| 13 | Changed coif (5) |
| 17 | Kind of warfare (8) |
| 18 | Driver's calculation (3) |
| 19 | Clearance (8) |
| 23 | Golden-___ (4) |
| 25 | Secretary of State (7) |
| 27 | Police command (6) |
| 29 | Beat keeper (7) |
| 30 | Non-coastal regions (7) |

## Down

| | |
|---|---|
| 1 | Warmed the bench, maybe (7) |
| 2 | Abbreviated cross words (4) |
| 3 | Put forth, as power or influence (5) |
| 4 | Start to melt (6) |
| 5 | Harbinger (4) |
| 6 | "Whoa there, buddy!" (9) |
| 10 | Photo (8) |
| 11 | Tropical fruit that is one of the flavors in Hawaiian Punch (6) |
| 14 | Manning with two Super Bowl wins (3) |
| 15 | Name related to Inga (4) |
| 16 | "Quo Vadis? "emperor (4) |
| 18 | "Better ___ ..." (3) |
| 20 | Speed skater and past "Dancing with the Star champ Apolo Anton ___ (4) |
| 21 | One of the guys (4) |
| 22 | Caviar source (6) |
| 24 | Offstage areas (5) |
| 25 | Branch road (4) |
| 26 | Eye sore (4) |
| 28 | Letter resembling a trident (3) |

# Samurai Sudoku 1

Samurai sudoku puzzles consist of five overlapping sudoku grids. The standard sudoku rules apply to each 9 x 9 grid. Place digits from 1 to 9 in each empty cell. Every row, every column, and every 3 x 3 box should contain one of each digit.

# Fallen Phrases 1

*Solve the puzzle.*

```
    G  E  T  S     E  E  O  M

 M  A  A  E  E  W  L  C  W  E  L  L

 T  N  A  I  S  R  I  I  T  W  E  A  T

 A  H  K  V  N  I  T  S  F  I  H  S  O
```

## Puzzle A

# Maze 3

*Solve the puzzle*

Start

End

# Cryptograms

*Solve the puzzles*

1. QPILG EPI SMGJF TZ SJZ JMG BIRHOAJHQ IK FJHZ

QPOHRL EPOBP GLBJXG QPILG EPI SMGJF IHYZ TZ

HORPQ. – GSRJM JYYJH XIG

Hint:

Q = T

2. FLV OTPC PE PN EL NPE KLVC EL VMPES VFSC ILQ FTOS

CLE NELLK QH EL XPOS. – FSCMI KTOPK EFLMSTQ

Hint:

E = T

# Nonograms

*Solve the puzzle.*

## Puzzle A

| | 1 4 1 | 2 5 | 4 1 | 4 1 1 | 3 2 1 | 1 3 1 | 2 2 2 | 1 7 | 1 1 2 1 | 1 1 2 3 |
|---|---|---|---|---|---|---|---|---|---|---|
| 2 1 3 | | | | | | | | | | |
| 1 2 1 | | | | | | | | | | |
| 8 | | | | | | | | | | |
| 2 1 | | | | | | | | | | |
| 4 1 1 | | | | | | | | | | |
| 3 6 | | | | | | | | | | |
| 2 6 | | | | | | | | | | |
| 2 1 1 1 | | | | | | | | | | |
| 1 1 2 1 | | | | | | | | | | |
| 1 2 2 2 | | | | | | | | | | |

## Puzzle B

| | 2 5 | 1 2 1 | 1 1 3 1 | 2 5 | 1 5 | 2 2 2 | 4 1 2 | 1 4 1 1 | 1 7 | 2 3 1 |
|---|---|---|---|---|---|---|---|---|---|---|
| 1 1 3 | | | | | | | | | | |
| 1 2 2 2 | | | | | | | | | | |
| 1 2 1 | | | | | | | | | | |
| 1 5 | | | | | | | | | | |
| 1 1 1 2 | | | | | | | | | | |
| 5 4 | | | | | | | | | | |
| 1 4 2 | | | | | | | | | | |
| 1 8 | | | | | | | | | | |
| 1 2 1 1 | | | | | | | | | | |
| 3 1 3 | | | | | | | | | | |

# Sudoku 4

*Solve the puzzle*

| 3 | 2 | 1 |   | 5 |   | 9 | 4 | 7 |
|---|---|---|---|---|---|---|---|---|
| 7 | 8 |   |   | 1 |   |   | 6 | 5 |
|   |   | 6 | 7 |   | 4 | 1 |   |   |
| 5 | 4 | 9 |   |   |   | 7 | 8 | 6 |
|   |   |   |   |   |   |   |   |   |
|   |   | 9 |   | 6 |   |   |   |   |
| 1 |   | 5 |   | 6 |   | 4 |   | 2 |
|   | 3 |   | 2 |   | 7 |   | 5 |   |
| 2 |   | 7 |   | 4 |   | 8 |   | 3 |

# Kakuro 2

*Solve the puzzle. The rules of Kakuro are simple - place the numbers 1 to 9 into the puzzle grid so that each continuous horizontal or vertical run of empty squares adds up to the value to the left of it or above it respectively. This value is shown either to the right or below a diagonal line.*

# Word Scramble 1

*Solve the puzzle. Unscramble the words.*

## Positive 5 letter words

1. egera _____

2. sibsl _____

3. vebar _____

4. lncea _____

5. hesrf _____

6. trega _____

7. lhuag _____

8. cluyk _____

9. qutei _____

10. hirtg _____

11. imles _____

12. opudr _____

13. vlita _____

14. strtu _____

15. loehw _____

# Spot the Difference 1

*Solve the puzzle. Find 9 differences. Circle each one.*

# Find the Pattern

*Solve the puzzle.* **Puzzle B**

## CHOOSE ANSWER

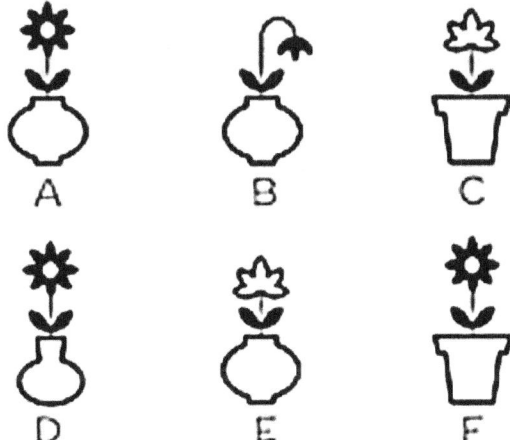

# Sudoku 5

*Solve the puzzle*

| | | | 6 | 9 | | 8 | | |
|---|---|---|---|---|---|---|---|---|
| | 7 | 4 | | 8 | 1 | 3 | 6 | |
| 8 | 1 | | 7 | | 5 | | 4 | |
| | 8 | 5 | | | | 7 | | 4 |
| 2 | 3 | | | | | | 8 | 6 |
| 4 | | 9 | | | | 5 | 2 | |
| | 9 | | 5 | | 3 | | 1 | 7 |
| | 4 | 1 | 9 | 7 | | 6 | 5 | |
| | | 2 | | 4 | 6 | | | |

# Maze 4

*Solve the puzzle*

Start

End

# Slice Puzzle 1

*Solve the puzzle. Draw each figure in the matching letter and number square below.*

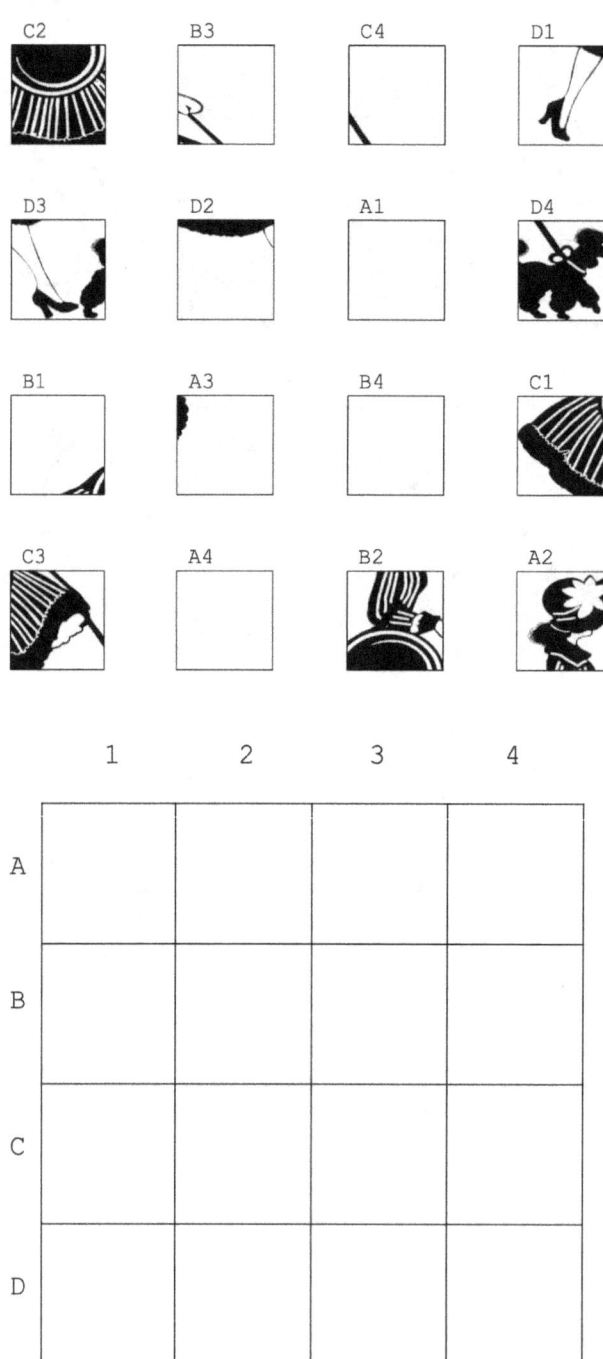

# Samurai Sudoku 2

Samurai sudoku puzzles consist of five overlapping sudoku grids. The standard sudoku rules apply to each 9 x 9 grid. Place digits from 1 to 9 in each empty cell. Every row, every column, and every 3 x 3 box should contain one of each digit.

# Sudoku 6

*Solve the puzzle*

| | 7 | | 4 | | 9 | | 1 | |
|---|---|---|---|---|---|---|---|---|
| | | | 3 | | 5 | | | |
| 6 | | | 8 | 1 | 2 | | | 3 |
| | 6 | 7 | | 8 | | 9 | 4 | |
| | | | 5 | 4 | 6 | | | |
| 1 | 4 | 3 | | | | 5 | 6 | 8 |
| | | 5 | | | | 4 | | |
| 8 | 3 | | 7 | 2 | 4 | | 5 | 9 |
| 4 | | 9 | | | | 2 | | 7 |

# Maze 5

*Solve the puzzle*

Start

End

# Word Fill-in

*Solve the puzzle.* **Puzzle 2**

- void
- wary
- whim
- gaudy
- mirth
- toxic
- quench
- robust
- sequel
- subtle
- invoice
- rupture
- vocation
- potential
- counterfeit

# Crossword 4

*Solve the puzzle*

### Across

1   Forte, in music (4)
3   Tooth doctor (7)
9   Name on Pisa's airport (7)

10  Olds model for six years (5)
11  Topper for a princess (5)
13  Suffix from the Russian (3)
15  S.C. summer hours (3)
17  Neither's tagalong (3)
18  Express Amtrak option (5)
21  "I'll believe it when I see it" (6)

23  Meadow mom (4)
25  Ice crust (4)
26  Hubbell of Cooperstown (4)
27  Retreat (8)
29  Mil. training center (3)
31  Dame of fame (4)
32  One trading in futures? (4)
34  Title for a Sevillian (5)
35  Barber formerly in the NFL and now on NBC (4)
36  Father of Æthelwulf (6)

### Down

1   Sales technique (11)
2   Advise strongly (4)
4   Mathematician once pictured on Swiss money (5)
5   The thing you're doing (4)
6   Offed (5)
7   Borneo seaport (4)
8   "Don Giovanni" soprano (6)
12  Is definitely not in the pink (4)
14  Midleg bones (8)
16  Many people get one in the summer (and so do this puzzle's theme entries) (3)
19  To ___ (perfectly) (5)
20  "I ___ it all to my teammates!" (3)
22  Bring on the market (7)
23  Asked for milk, in a way (5)
24  Corporate hustle and bustle (7)
28  Drub (5)
30  G.I. carrier (3)
31  Benevolent brothers' animal (3)
33  Serpent's prey (3)

# Cryptograms

*Solve the puzzles*

3. GCBFNWVYW PBDWX, RHI FEXVBD NECYWKX. –

SNMKWV IWCCAXBC

Hint:

X = S

4. YMQW CDYPV NDY NOQQ HOPL FYOMF CYY TBH KBM

ZYPPOGQW TOMJ YSC DYN TBH YMV KBM FY.- C. P. VQOYC

Hint:

G = B

# Math Squares

*Solve the puzzle.*

| | + | | / | | - | | **-7** |
|---|---|---|---|---|---|---|---|
| + | ■ | + | ■ | × | ■ | / | |
| | + | | + | | / | | **13** |
| - | ■ | - | ■ | / | ■ | + | |
| | + | | - | | - | | **10** |
| - | ■ | + | ■ | × | ■ | - | |
| | + | | - | | + | | **26** |
| **-1** | | **5** | | **24** | | **1** | |

**Puzzle C**

# Crossword 5

*Solve the puzzle*

| # | Across |
|---|---|
| 1 | "MASH" character (5) |
| 4 | Arthur Hailey work (5) |
| 7 | Crowd (9) |
| 9 | Grimm heroine (7) |
| 12 | Bundle of twigs used for fuel (6) |
| 14 | Military depot (7) |
| 16 | "Believe" pop star whose name sounds like a Facebook option (4) |
| 18 | Metal (3) |
| 20 | Fireplace tool (5) |
| 21 | Kahlúa and cream over ice (8) |
| 23 | Egyptian queen of gods (4) |
| 25 | Shipwrecked Shakespearean sorcerer (8) |
| 27 | Green jam ingredient? (6) |
| 28 | Spring feasts (7) |
| 29 | Adjusts to change (6) |

| # | Down |
|---|---|
| 1 | Chopper blades (6) |
| 2 | Less than 90° (5) |
| 3 | Cowboy-boot accessory (4) |
| 4 | Howling scavenger (5) |
| 5 | Distance (6) |
| 6 | 2013 Ryan Reynolds/Jeff Bridges movie about afterlife cops (4) |
| 8 | Exhorting individual (5) |
| 10 | Tension-building part of an at bat (9) |
| 11 | End of the end of October? (3) |
| 12 | Unidentifiable (8) |
| 13 | Of gums (3) |
| 15 | Organs for listening (4) |
| 17 | Hundred Acre Wood pessimist (6) |
| 19 | Emollients (7) |
| 20 | Snow-packed trail (5) |
| 22 | Towboats' burdens (6) |
| 24 | Volcanic stream (4) |
| 26 | Rose up 15,890 times in 24 years (4) |

# Word Search 4

*Solve the puzzle*

```
L M N X F C N C Y R S K C E N N U Z G U
S U F O W L O Z I B G O C L O T H E S Z
I F F R I N M L W T N E N O P M O C W U
T D X D F T V T C E P S O R P B L F O P
E V P R N F A L I R P N O I T I D D A L
Z W O G R A V R S C I T I L O P P Q U A
Q N N E R T H P B S N R N P D T R B C C
T V N Y K Y L E M E R T X E A E I X D I
E C J A H W V D S P L Y W J E M S P G D
H V G Q F A B D G Q B E F C H P O O O E
M T S X E B E R A R M F C N A E N L T M
J N T L F L A C S N I H T I W R E L H O
B M P M A I U J Y D L W A I T A R W E N
R R V M N D L R J L C W T U T T R H R T
B E R S E C N E U Q E S N O C U P O W H
H O T K U Y F G K D E S E R T R C M I E
N D D L T A E H E E Q O J G G E Y V S X
P L J V A C N T T N A R G I M M I Z E L
K Q J W I C Z L T X Y R O M E M G T Y H
T U O H S I N N O C E N T O E G G F K M
```

| ADDITION | GRAIN | POLITICS |
|----------|-------|----------|
| AHEAD | HANDFUL | POLL |
| ALTER | HEAT | PRISONER |
| CELEBRATION | IMMIGRANT | PROSPECT |
| CLIMB | INNOCENT | RARE |
| CLOTHES | LEAVE | SHOUT |
| COMPONENT | MEDICAL | SITE |
| CONFRONT | MEMORY | TEMPERATURE |
| CONSEQUENCE | MONTH | WAIT |
| DESERT | NECK | WHOM |
| EXTREMELY | NORMAL | WITHIN |
| FRENCH | OTHERWISE | |

# Kakuro 3

*Solve the puzzle. The rules of Kakuro are simple - place the numbers 1 to 9 into the puzzle grid so that each continuous horizontal or vertical run of empty squares adds up to the value to the left of it or above it respectively. This value is shown either to the right or below a diagonal line.*

# Word Fill-in

*Solve the puzzle.* **Puzzle 1**

- grim
- wince
- wrath
- yearn
- astute
- resume
- tragedy
- upright
- vicious
- authentic
- negligent
- predatory
- unscathed
- incredulous
- substantial

# Word Puzzles
## *Matching Duos*

*Match the two words that are commonly used together*

| | | | |
|---|---|---|---|
| 1. | mom | a. | brimstone |
| 2. | divide | b. | stripes |
| 3. | fire | c. | Englishman |
| 4. | rock | d. | pop |
| 5. | war | e. | ivory |
| 6. | skull | f. | phloem |
| 7. | death | g. | answer |
| 8. | question | h. | conquer |
| 9. | stars | i. | taxes |
| 10. | motherhood | j. | jetsam |
| 11. | flotsam | k. | hard place |
| 12. | ebony | l. | apple pie |
| 13. | xylem | m. | peace |
| 14. | mad dogs | n. | bones |

# Word Search 6

## Solve the puzzle

```
C F O U N D A T I O N M R O T A C U D E
O U N V O C H E D L L A R E V O M E V I
N A A E U H G E N B P M I E E P A C S E
S S E U G I T B X O A K E T Y M T K Z V
E N G C F L I A O E L U N A B L E G P E
N O Y O D D N T V T X A Z M S J B I K A
S H R M B H S H Q A P P R E C I A T E U
U E E M C O T R K O S B Y B L A I C O S
S E V A T O R O E Q Y L L A I C E P S E
O D O N E D U O B R E C O M M E N D P G
T I C D R X C M I W A D N E G A E Q Q E
O H S C M H T C Y M E T A R E P S E D N
W E I H S F I O T E C S C O V F E O T E
A U D A E F O F I L T P L O T S W B X R
R S R T J Y N F R E S R E S E M B L E A
D D Q B T D Z E B C R O V R L O M R P T
S L C H A R G E E T I Y T C I Q J W A I
M O I L J N M V L X F E Q X O T O E E O
P C K N A T T V E J P I O C E A A N H N
T A G N O S H I C F D G G R B N F K C X
```

| | | | |
|---|---|---|---|
| AGENDA | COMMAND | GENERATION | SONG |
| ALONE | CONSENSUS | GUESS | TANK |
| APPRECIATE | DESPERATE | HIDE | TERMS |
| BATHROOM | DISCOVERY | INSTRUCTION | TOWARDS |
| CELEBRITY | EDUCATOR | LOTS | UNABLE |
| CHARGE | ELECT | NEXT | URBAN |
| CHEAP | ESCAPE | OVERALL | |
| CHILDHOOD | ESPECIALLY | RECOMMEND | |
| COFFEE | FIRST | RESEMBLE | |
| COLD | FOUNDATION | SOCIAL | |

# Odd One Out 2

*Find the one that is different.*

# Samurai Sudoku 3

Samurai sudoku puzzles consist of five overlapping sudoku grids. The standard sudoku rules apply to each 9 x 9 grid. Place digits from 1 to 9 in each empty cell. Every row, every column, and every 3 x 3 box should contain one of each digit.

# Cryptograms

*Solve the puzzles*

5. S GSHTO KUERXO KD PVO QODP HOEKLO MRH

VSLLKUODD K OYOH VOSHB RM.- ISUO SFDPOU

Hint:

D = S


6. YUCBC XBC PNNRM NJ TUGLU YUC PXLRM XKI LNSCBM

XBC PE JXB YUC PCMY VXBYM. - LUXBWCM IGLRCKM

Hint:

X = A

# Word Scramble 1

*Solve the puzzle. Unscramble the words.*

## Virtues

1. egsryneiot

2. cgrea

3. aesgruiossen

4. edtiagutr

5. eulsnhpefsl

6. nhsyteo

7. ohorn

8. iitmyuhl

9. sekdnnis

10. salmidei

11. imtpartliyia

12. uslsfnoejy

13. neinoncec

14. etiitgym

15. laytoly

# Fallen Phrases 2

*Solve the puzzle.*

```
            S           B
  I  T     O  U  T  N  O  U     T
  I  H  E  T  L  N  S  R  S  R  I  O
  T  E  H  O  I  R  A  O  T  U  E  N
  D  N  S  I  S  D  Y  E  L  V  T  S
```

## Puzzle B

# Fallen Phrases 4

*Solve the puzzle.*

```
  H W P     P       S   T         I         L F   Y O       E P   L           I T
D G R A     P U S B U E D         M S A     A W I T S U     L Y L W       Y O U
H A E N S N E I S T I S     H S A H     I L A G H R B U Y O N D I C U
W O P N I Q U R E U L Y W A I C Y A B U T Y E T F W I O N H S O H R
```

## Puzzle D

# Spot the Difference 2

*Solve the puzzle. Find 9 differences. Circle each one.*

# Number Blocks

*Solve the puzzles.*

## Puzzle C

|       |       |       |       |       |
|-------|-------|-------|-------|-------|
|       |       |       |       | **16** |
|       |       | 3     |       | 16    |
|       |       |       |       | 20    |
|       | 7     |       | 6     | 20    |
| 8     |       |       |       | 22    |
| 26    | 24    | 15    | 13    | 21    |

**Puzzle C**

## Puzzle D

|       |       |       |       |       |
|-------|-------|-------|-------|-------|
|       |       |       |       | **19** |
|       | 9     |       |       | 20    |
|       |       | 5     |       | 20    |
|       |       |       | 0     | 6     |
| 7     | 4     |       | 9     | 26    |
| 21    | 18    | 13    | 20    | 20    |

**Puzzle D**

# Math Squares

*Solve the puzzle.*

| | + | | − | | + | | **16** |
|---|---|---|---|---|---|---|---|
| + | ■ | + | ■ | − | ■ | + | |
| | × | | + | | − | | **15** |
| + | ■ | + | ■ | + | ■ | − | |
| | − | | − | | + | | **−5** |
| − | ■ | + | ■ | + | ■ | / | |
| | + | | − | | / | | **4** |
| **10** | | **25** | | **27** | | **3** | |

**Puzzle B**

# Nonograms

*Solve the puzzle.*

### Puzzle C

| | 3 1 1 2 | 2 1 2 1 | 1 3 1 | 3 2 1 3 | 4 5 | 1 4 | 2 4 3 | 7 1 | 2 2 4 | 2 1 | 4 2 1 | 3 1 4 |
|---|---|---|---|---|---|---|---|---|---|---|---|---|
| 2 1 2 1 | | | | | | | | | | | | |
| 2 2 1 4 | | | | | | | | | | | | |
| 1 2 1 2 | | | | | | | | | | | | |
| 4 2 | | | | | | | | | | | | |
| 1 6 1 | | | | | | | | | | | | |
| 1 1 5 1 | | | | | | | | | | | | |
| 4 1 | | | | | | | | | | | | |
| 3 1 1 | | | | | | | | | | | | |
| 3 1 2 1 | | | | | | | | | | | | |
| 4 3 2 | | | | | | | | | | | | |
| 1 2 1 1 1 | | | | | | | | | | | | |
| 5 3 1 | | | | | | | | | | | | |

### Puzzle D

| | 1 1 2 1 | 7 3 | 2 1 2 | 8 1 | 2 1 1 1 | 4 3 1 | 1 2 3 1 | 1 1 2 1 | 5 2 1 | 4 2 2 | 2 2 2 1 | 1 1 5 |
|---|---|---|---|---|---|---|---|---|---|---|---|---|
| 2 1 1 2 | | | | | | | | | | | | |
| 1 1 6 | | | | | | | | | | | | |
| 5 2 | | | | | | | | | | | | |
| 11 | | | | | | | | | | | | |
| 2 1 1 3 | | | | | | | | | | | | |
| 1 1 1 1 | | | | | | | | | | | | |
| 1 6 1 | | | | | | | | | | | | |
| 2 2 4 | | | | | | | | | | | | |
| 1 1 1 3 | | | | | | | | | | | | |
| 2 2 1 | | | | | | | | | | | | |
| 2 5 | | | | | | | | | | | | |
| 5 1 1 | | | | | | | | | | | | |

# Slice Puzzle 3

*Solve the puzzle. Draw each figure in the matching letter and number square below.*

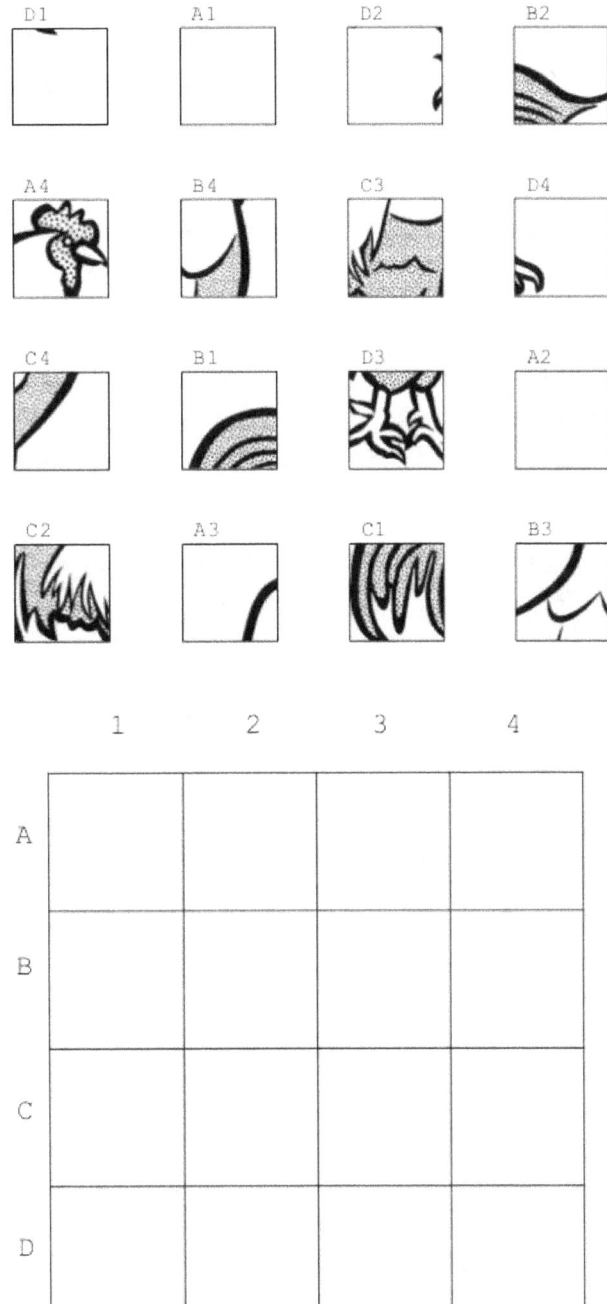

# Word Search 5

*Solve the puzzle*

```
E T E K X M O R T G A G E S A N J N W V
E H N D C L T B X O A R M E D N C E U F
E L G N I S M I L E E V I T A E R C A L
R L G U Y T I M P O R T A N C E P D A C
I A E S O J I Z G B T F M P X K B Y V S
T H S X P R O O S Q K A Y E K R S O G K
E S T A I R H X N S U C J K A B M T V V
R U H Q O X V T P E T T O N B A E H K P
C H A R T H L U R L U N C V J A R A E E
Y A P P A R E N T L Y H E B D R E I E E
Q W I M I Q D T S N Y R I M U L B R H N
J V N M V S J O O W A D I R T M Q O C I
S Q Z Z P M Q W T D I R O I X S T E S A
R S O L Y O H X R O E G W D J P E C A T
E G T J L E S A E W H J G E R U O V A E
D D H G R X S E F P Z P E U F I Z R N R
N F E E O I O E F C E S O P M O C U C I
O K R T M P F H I D Y L U R T N O M G H
W N Y Q G C T W D C S C I G A R E T T E
B M S E N A T E V N O I T A L U G E R V
```

| | | | |
|---|---|---|---|
| ADMIRE | DARE | NOWHERE | SHALL |
| APPARENTLY | DIFFER | OTHER | SMILE |
| ARMED | EDITION | PHOTO | SOFT |
| BRANCH | HAIR | PORCH | STAIR |
| CHART | IMPORTANCE | REGULATION | THROUGH |
| CHEEK | IMPOSE | RETAIN | TRULY |
| CIGARETTE | INVESTMENT | RETIRE | WONDER |
| COMPOSE | MERE | RIDE | |
| CREATIVE | MORTGAGE | SENATE | |

# Odd One Out 3

*Find the one that is different.*

# Puzzle Solutions

# Nonogram Solution Puzzle A

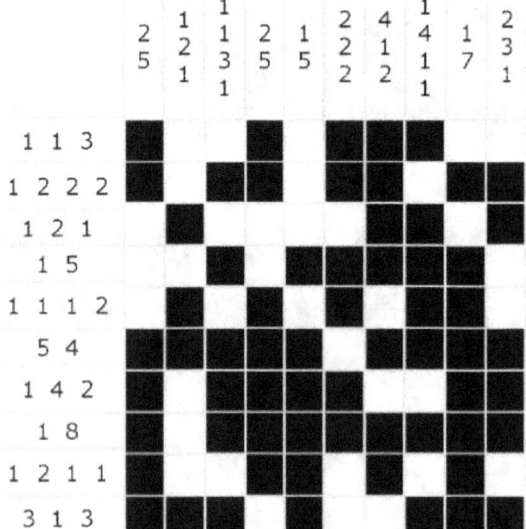

# Nonogram Solution Puzzle B

## Math Squares Solution Puzzle A

| 6 | × | 8 | + | 1 | / | 7 | 7 |
|---|---|---|---|---|---|---|---|
| - |  | - |  | - |  | + |  |
| 5 | - | 11 | + | 9 | × | 10 | 30 |
| × |  | - |  | / |  | + |  |
| 4 | - | 14 | / | 2 | + | 15 | 10 |
| × |  | - |  | + |  | / |  |
| 13 | + | 12 | - | 3 | + | 16 | 38 |
| 52 |  | -29 |  | -1 |  | 2 |  |

## Math Squares Solution Puzzle B

| 7 | + | 4 | - | 10 | + | 15 | 16 |
|---|---|---|---|---|---|---|---|
| + |  | + |  | - |  | + |  |
| 5 | × | 1 | + | 12 | - | 2 | 15 |
| + |  | + |  | + |  | - |  |
| 9 | - | 6 | - | 16 | + | 8 | -5 |
| - |  | + |  | + |  | / |  |
| 11 | + | 14 | - | 13 | / | 3 | 4 |
| 10 |  | 25 |  | 27 |  | 3 |  |

## Math Squares Solution Puzzle C

| 9 | + | 1 | / | 2 | - | 12 | -7 |
|---|---|---|---|---|---|---|---|
| + |  | + |  | × |  | / |  |
| 10 | + | 14 | + | 15 | / | 3 | 13 |
| - |  | - |  | / |  | + |  |
| 7 | + | 16 | - | 5 | - | 8 | 10 |
| - |  | + |  | × |  | - |  |
| 13 | + | 6 | - | 4 | + | 11 | 26 |
| -1 |  | 5 |  | 24 |  | 1 |  |

# Number Blocks

|   |   |   |   | 6  |
|---|---|---|---|----|

| 6 | 8 | 3 | 4 | 21 |
|---|---|---|---|----|
| 6 | 2 | 0 | 6 | 14 |
| 1 | 0 | 5 | 5 | 11 |
| 2 | 3 | 4 | 2 | 11 |
| 15 | 13 | 12 | 17 | 15 |

Solution Puzzle A

|   |   |   |   | 16 |
|---|---|---|---|----|

| 6 | 7 | 3 | 0 | 16 |
|---|---|---|---|----|
| 8 | 8 | 1 | 3 | 20 |
| 4 | 7 | 3 | 6 | 20 |
| 8 | 2 | 8 | 4 | 22 |
| 26 | 24 | 15 | 13 | 21 |

Solution Puzzle C

|   |   |   |   | 17 |
|---|---|---|---|----|

| 6 | 6 | 7 | 2 | 21 |
|---|---|---|---|----|
| 3 | 2 | 4 | 5 | 14 |
| 7 | 6 | 3 | 5 | 21 |
| 5 | 0 | 7 | 6 | 18 |
| 21 | 14 | 21 | 18 | 17 |

Solution Puzzle B

|   |   |   |   | 19 |
|---|---|---|---|----|

| 8 | 9 | 0 | 3 | 20 |
|---|---|---|---|----|
| 6 | 1 | 5 | 8 | 20 |
| 0 | 4 | 2 | 0 | 6  |
| 7 | 4 | 6 | 9 | 26 |
| 21 | 18 | 13 | 20 | 20 |

Solution Puzzle D

# Samurai Sudoku

## Puzzle 1

Top-left grid:
```
7 9 6 2 3 8 5 1 4
4 1 5 9 7 6 3 8 2
2 3 8 5 4 1 6 7 9
6 4 9 1 8 5 2 3 7
1 8 2 7 6 3 4 9 5
5 7 3 4 2 9 8 6 1
9 6 1 8 5 4 7 2 3
8 5 7 3 9 2 1 4 6
3 2 4 6 1 7 9 5 8
```

Top-right grid:
```
7 8 6 2 1 5 4 9 3
2 3 4 9 7 6 5 1 8
9 1 5 4 8 3 7 2 6
8 6 3 7 5 2 1 4 9
4 2 9 8 6 1 3 5 7
5 7 1 3 9 4 6 8 2
1 9 8 6 4 7 2 3 5
3 5 7 1 2 9 8 6 4
6 4 2 5 3 8 9 7 1
```

Center grid:
```
7 2 3 4 5 6 1 9 8
1 4 6 8 9 2 3 5 7
9 5 8 1 3 7 6 4 2
6 1 5 2 4 8 9 7 3
8 3 7 9 6 5 2 1 4
2 9 4 3 7 1 8 6 5
3 7 9 6 2 4 5 8 1
4 8 2 5 1 9 7 3 6
5 6 1 7 8 3 4 2 9
```

Bottom-left grid:
```
5 1 8 2 6 4 3 7 9
9 3 6 7 5 1 4 8 2
4 7 2 9 3 8 5 6 1
1 4 7 3 2 9 8 5 6
2 6 9 8 4 5 1 3 7
8 5 3 6 1 7 2 9 4
7 9 1 5 8 2 6 4 3
3 8 4 1 9 6 7 2 5
6 2 5 4 7 3 9 1 8
```

Bottom-right grid:
```
5 8 1 4 2 3 7 6 9
7 3 6 5 1 9 4 2 8
4 2 9 8 7 6 3 1 5
1 4 7 3 9 5 6 8 2
6 9 2 7 8 1 5 3 4
8 5 3 6 4 2 1 9 7
2 1 4 9 3 7 8 5 6
9 6 8 1 5 4 2 7 3
3 7 5 2 6 8 9 4 1
```

## Puzzle 2

Top-left grid:
```
6 2 7 4 9 1 5 3 8
5 4 3 6 8 2 9 1 7
9 1 8 7 5 3 4 6 2
7 8 1 3 2 9 6 4 5
4 5 2 1 6 8 3 7 9
3 9 6 5 4 7 8 2 1
1 7 9 8 3 4 2 5 6
2 3 5 9 1 6 7 8 4
8 6 4 2 7 5 1 9 3
```

Top-right grid:
```
1 2 5 7 4 6 8 3 9
7 9 3 5 2 8 1 4 6
8 6 4 3 1 9 5 7 2
3 8 1 4 7 2 6 9 5
6 4 9 8 5 3 7 2 1
2 5 7 6 9 1 3 8 4
9 1 8 2 6 7 4 5 3
5 3 2 1 8 4 9 6 7
4 7 6 9 3 5 2 1 8
```

Center grid:
```
2 5 6 7 3 4 9 1 8
7 8 4 6 9 1 5 3 2
1 9 3 2 8 5 4 7 6
5 1 7 3 2 8 6 9 4
9 4 8 1 5 6 3 2 7
6 3 2 9 4 7 8 5 1
8 6 9 5 7 2 1 4 3
3 2 1 4 6 9 7 8 5
4 7 5 8 1 3 2 6 9
```

Bottom-left grid:
```
5 1 3 7 2 4 8 6 9
4 7 6 5 9 8 3 2 1
2 9 8 1 6 3 4 7 5
1 3 7 2 8 9 6 5 4
9 4 5 3 1 6 2 8 7
8 6 2 4 5 7 9 1 3
6 5 4 9 7 2 1 3 8
3 8 1 6 4 5 7 9 2
7 2 9 8 3 1 5 4 6
```

Bottom-right grid:
```
1 4 3 9 6 2 5 7 8
7 8 5 1 3 4 2 9 6
2 6 9 5 7 8 4 1 3
5 7 6 2 9 1 3 8 4
4 9 2 7 8 3 1 6 5
8 3 1 4 5 6 9 2 7
3 2 7 6 1 5 8 4 9
6 1 8 3 4 9 7 5 2
9 5 4 8 2 7 6 3 1
```

## Puzzle 3

Top-left grid:
```
3 5 7 4 2 1 9 6 8
6 2 1 8 9 3 5 4 7
4 9 8 6 7 5 3 2 1
2 8 6 9 4 7 1 5 3
7 4 3 5 1 8 6 9 2
9 1 5 3 6 2 8 7 4
8 3 2 7 5 6 4 1 9
5 7 4 1 3 9 2 8 6
1 6 9 2 8 4 7 3 5
```

Top-right grid:
```
4 1 2 9 3 5 8 6 7
7 6 8 4 1 2 5 9 3
5 3 9 7 8 6 2 1 4
8 4 3 2 9 1 7 5 6
1 2 7 6 5 4 9 3 8
9 5 6 8 7 3 1 4 2
6 8 5 3 2 9 4 7 1
3 7 1 5 4 8 6 2 9
2 9 4 1 6 7 3 8 5
```

Center grid:
```
4 1 9 2 3 7 6 8 5
2 8 6 4 5 9 3 7 1
7 3 5 1 6 8 2 9 4
5 2 4 9 7 1 8 3 6
3 6 7 8 4 5 1 2 9
1 9 8 6 2 3 4 5 7
8 4 3 7 9 6 5 1 2
6 7 1 5 8 2 9 4 3
9 5 2 3 1 4 7 6 8
```

Bottom-left grid:
```
5 1 7 9 2 6 8 4 3
9 2 8 4 3 5 6 7 1
6 4 3 7 1 8 9 5 2
1 3 4 2 5 9 7 6 8
2 6 9 8 7 4 1 3 5
7 8 5 3 6 1 2 9 4
8 7 2 5 9 3 4 1 6
4 5 6 1 8 7 3 2 9
3 9 1 6 4 2 5 8 7
```

Bottom-right grid:
```
5 1 2 4 9 8 7 6 3
9 4 3 5 7 6 2 8 1
7 6 8 3 1 2 5 4 9
4 2 5 9 3 7 8 1 6
1 7 6 8 4 5 9 3 2
8 3 9 6 2 1 4 7 5
2 5 1 7 6 4 3 9 8
6 9 4 2 8 3 1 5 7
3 8 7 1 5 9 6 2 4
```

# Sudoku

**1**

| 7 | 2 | 3 | 8 | 4 | 6 | 1 | 5 | 9 |
|---|---|---|---|---|---|---|---|---|
| 6 | 1 | 5 | 3 | 9 | 2 | 4 | 7 | 8 |
| 8 | 4 | 9 | 7 | 1 | 5 | 6 | 3 | 2 |
| 3 | 7 | 8 | 6 | 5 | 4 | 9 | 2 | 1 |
| 1 | 9 | 4 | 2 | 8 | 7 | 3 | 6 | 5 |
| 2 | 5 | 6 | 9 | 3 | 1 | 8 | 4 | 7 |
| 5 | 6 | 1 | 4 | 7 | 9 | 2 | 8 | 3 |
| 4 | 8 | 7 | 1 | 2 | 3 | 5 | 9 | 6 |
| 9 | 3 | 2 | 5 | 6 | 8 | 7 | 1 | 4 |

**2**

| 3 | 2 | 7 | 1 | 5 | 8 | 9 | 4 | 6 |
|---|---|---|---|---|---|---|---|---|
| 6 | 1 | 9 | 4 | 3 | 7 | 5 | 8 | 2 |
| 5 | 4 | 8 | 9 | 6 | 2 | 7 | 1 | 3 |
| 1 | 8 | 6 | 5 | 7 | 4 | 3 | 2 | 9 |
| 4 | 3 | 2 | 6 | 8 | 9 | 1 | 5 | 7 |
| 9 | 7 | 5 | 3 | 2 | 1 | 4 | 6 | 8 |
| 7 | 6 | 4 | 2 | 1 | 3 | 8 | 9 | 5 |
| 8 | 5 | 1 | 7 | 9 | 6 | 2 | 3 | 4 |
| 2 | 9 | 3 | 8 | 4 | 5 | 6 | 7 | 1 |

**3**

| 1 | 5 | 3 | 8 | 4 | 7 | 6 | 2 | 9 |
|---|---|---|---|---|---|---|---|---|
| 9 | 4 | 8 | 2 | 6 | 1 | 5 | 3 | 7 |
| 7 | 6 | 2 | 3 | 5 | 9 | 8 | 1 | 4 |
| 2 | 7 | 5 | 6 | 9 | 3 | 4 | 8 | 1 |
| 8 | 1 | 4 | 7 | 2 | 5 | 3 | 9 | 6 |
| 6 | 3 | 9 | 4 | 1 | 8 | 7 | 5 | 2 |
| 5 | 2 | 6 | 9 | 3 | 4 | 1 | 7 | 8 |
| 4 | 8 | 1 | 5 | 7 | 2 | 9 | 6 | 3 |
| 3 | 9 | 7 | 1 | 8 | 6 | 2 | 4 | 5 |

**4**

| 3 | 2 | 1 | 6 | 5 | 8 | 9 | 4 | 7 |
|---|---|---|---|---|---|---|---|---|
| 7 | 8 | 4 | 3 | 1 | 9 | 2 | 6 | 5 |
| 9 | 5 | 6 | 7 | 2 | 4 | 1 | 3 | 8 |
| 5 | 4 | 9 | 1 | 3 | 2 | 7 | 8 | 6 |
| 6 | 7 | 2 | 4 | 8 | 5 | 3 | 1 | 9 |
| 8 | 1 | 3 | 9 | 7 | 6 | 5 | 2 | 4 |
| 1 | 9 | 5 | 8 | 6 | 3 | 4 | 7 | 2 |
| 4 | 3 | 8 | 2 | 9 | 7 | 6 | 5 | 1 |
| 2 | 6 | 7 | 5 | 4 | 1 | 8 | 9 | 3 |

**5**

| 5 | 2 | 3 | 6 | 9 | 4 | 8 | 7 | 1 |
|---|---|---|---|---|---|---|---|---|
| 9 | 7 | 4 | 2 | 8 | 1 | 3 | 6 | 5 |
| 8 | 1 | 6 | 7 | 3 | 5 | 2 | 4 | 9 |
| 1 | 8 | 5 | 3 | 6 | 2 | 7 | 9 | 4 |
| 2 | 3 | 7 | 4 | 5 | 9 | 1 | 8 | 6 |
| 4 | 6 | 9 | 8 | 1 | 7 | 5 | 2 | 3 |
| 6 | 9 | 8 | 5 | 2 | 3 | 4 | 1 | 7 |
| 3 | 4 | 1 | 9 | 7 | 8 | 6 | 5 | 2 |
| 7 | 5 | 2 | 1 | 4 | 6 | 9 | 3 | 8 |

**6**

| 3 | 7 | 2 | 4 | 6 | 9 | 8 | 1 | 5 |
|---|---|---|---|---|---|---|---|---|
| 9 | 8 | 1 | 3 | 7 | 5 | 6 | 2 | 4 |
| 6 | 5 | 4 | 8 | 1 | 2 | 7 | 9 | 3 |
| 5 | 6 | 7 | 1 | 8 | 3 | 9 | 4 | 2 |
| 2 | 9 | 8 | 5 | 4 | 6 | 3 | 7 | 1 |
| 1 | 4 | 3 | 2 | 9 | 7 | 5 | 6 | 8 |
| 7 | 2 | 5 | 9 | 3 | 1 | 4 | 8 | 6 |
| 8 | 3 | 6 | 7 | 2 | 4 | 1 | 5 | 9 |
| 4 | 1 | 9 | 6 | 5 | 8 | 2 | 3 | 7 |

## Fallen Phrases

A. Quote by Emily Dickenson -- That it will never come again is what makes life so sweet

B. Quote by William Shakespeare -- It is not in the stars to hold our destiny but in ourselves.

C. Quote by Sojourner Truth -- I feel safe in the midst of my enemies, for the truth is all powerful and will prevail

D. Quote by Nathaniel Hawthorne -- Happiness is as a butterfly which, when pursued, is always beyond our grasp, but which if you will sit down quietly, may alight upon you.

## Letter Tiles

A. We loved with a love that was more than love - Edgar Allan Poe

B. It was the best of times, it was the worst of times - Charles Dickens

C. Everyone thinks of changing the world, but no one thinks of changing himself - Leo Tolstoy

## Find the Pattern

Puzzle A – Answer: E

Puzzle B – Answer: D

## CRYPTOGRAM SOLUTIONS

1. Those who dream by day are cognizant of many things which escape those who dream only by night. – Edgar Allan Poe

2. How vain it is to sit down to write when you have not stood up to live. – Henry David Thoreau

3. Knowledge comes, but wisdom lingers. – Alfred Tennyson

4. Only those who will risk going too far can possibly find out how far one can go.- T. S. Eliot

5. A large income is the best recipe for happiness I ever heard of.- Jane Austen

6. There are books of which the backs and covers are by far the best parts. - Charles Dickens

# Spot the difference

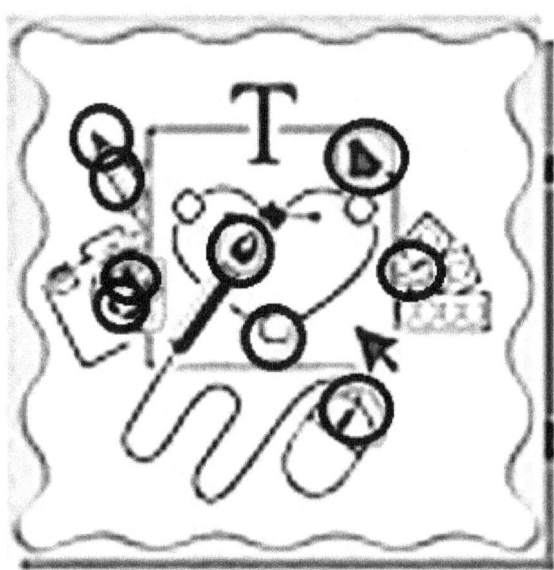

## Puzzle 1

### Across
1 Forte, in music (4)
3 Tooth doctor (7)
9 Name on Pisa's airport (7)
10 Olds model for six years (5)
11 Topper for a princess (5)
13 Suffix from the Russian (3)
15 S.C. summer hours (3)
18 Express Amtrak option (5)
21 "I'll believe it when I see it" (6)
23 Meadow mom (4)
25 Ice crust (4)
26 Hubbell of Cooperstown (4)
27 Retreat (8)
29 Mil. training center (3)
31 Dame of fame (4)
32 One trading in futures? (4)
34 Title for a Sevillian (5)
35 Barber formerly in the NFL and now on NBC (4)
36 Father of Æthelwulf (6)

### Down
1 Sales technique (11)
2 Advise strongly (4)
4 Mathematician once pictured on Swiss money (5)
5 The thing you're doing (4)
6 Offed (5)
7 Borneo seaport (4)
8 "Don Giovanni" soprano (6)
12 Is definitely not in the pink (4)
14 Midleg bones (8)
16 Many people get one in the summer (and so do this puzzle's theme entries) (3)
19 To ___ (perfectly) (5)
20 "I ___ it all to my teammates!" (3)
22 Bring on the market (7)
23 Asked for milk, in a way (5)
24 Corporate hustle and bustle (7)
28 Drub (5)
30 G.I. carrier (3)
31 Benevolent brothers' animal (3)
33 Serpent's prey (3)

## Puzzle 2

### Across
1 "MASH" character (5)
4 Arthur Hailey work (5)
7 Crowd (9)
9 Grimm heroine (7)
12 Bundle of twigs used for fuel (6)
14 Military depot (7)
16 "Believe" pop star whose name sounds like a Facebook option (4)
18 Metal (3)
20 Fireplace tool (5)
21 Kahlúa and cream over ice (8)
23 Egyptian queen of gods (4)
25 Shipwrecked Shakespearean sorcerer (8)
27 Green jam ingredient? (6)
28 Spring feasts (7)
29 Adjusts to change (6)

### Down
1 Chopper blades (6)
2 Less than 90° (5)
3 Cowboy-boot accessory (4)
4 Howling scavenger (5)
5 Distance (6)
6 2013 Ryan Reynolds/Jeff Bridges movie about afterlife cops (4)
8 Exhorting individual (7)
10 Tension-building part of an at bat (9)
11 End of the end of October? (3)
12 Unidentifiable (8)
13 Of gums (3)
15 Organs for listening (4)
17 Hundred Acre Wood pessimist (6)
19 Emollients (7)
20 Snow-packed trail (5)
22 Towboats' burdens (6)
24 Volcanic stream (4)
26 Rose up 15,890 times in 24 years (4)

## Puzzle 3

### Across
1 "Raiders of the Lost Ark" movie genre (15)
8 Atrocity (7)
9 Without creating disarray (6)
11 Motown celebrity (5)
13 Said of an active person (7)
14 Chicken-King separator (3)
16 Communication means at the office (9)
18 Confident crossword solver's choice (3)
20 Type of lab (3)
21 Capone's political position? (9)
24 Horseplayer's letters (3)
25 Kesey and Berry (4)
27 Pharmacists notations (7)
29 Cake toppers (5)
30 Actor who said "Only the gentle are ever really strong" (9)

### Down
1 ___ santé (French toast) (6)
2 Duke or dame (5)
3 'Is it a boy/girl?' (3)
4 'Am so!' retort (6)
5 Shrew (6)
6 Human-shaped mug (4)
7 Cast again (7)
10 Bedfordshire town and airport (5)
12 Plunder (4)
14 Curry taken in the morning (3)
15 Sit-down occasion (4)
17 Kind of sampling (6)
18 Like something that's going around? (7)
19 C.I.A. (3)
20 What Ben Adhem did (7)
22 Connects with a memory (6)
23 "Napoleon" director Gance (4)
26 Coming and going spots (4)
28 Grenade activator (3)

## Across

1. Whether to aim at 7 or 10, in bowling? (13)
7. Biblical movie in the making, in wide screen. (7)
8. They're too often inflated (4)
9. ___ one's laurels (6)
12. Long and narrow (6)
13. Changed coif (5)
17. Kind of warfare (8)
18. Driver's calculation (3)
19. Clearance (8)
23. Golden-___ (4)
25. Secretary of State (7)
27. Police command (6)
29. Beat keeper (7)
30. Non-coastal regions (7)

## Down

1. Warmed the bench, maybe (7)
2. Abbreviated cross words (4)
3. Put forth, as power or influence (5)
4. Start to melt (6)
5. Harbinger (4)
6. "Whoa there, buddy!" (9)
10. Photo (8)
11. Tropical fruit that is one of the flavors in Hawaiian Punch (6)
14. Manning with two Super Bowl wins (3)
15. Name related to Inga (4)
16. "Quo Vadis? "emperor (4)
18. "Better ___ ..." (3)
20. Speed skater and past "Dancing with the Star champ Apolo Anton ___ (4)
21. One of the guys (4)
22. Caviar source (6)
24. Offstage areas (5)
25. Branch road (4)
26. Eye sore (4)
28. Letter resembling a trident (3)

## Across

1. Whether to aim at 7 or 10, in bowling? (13)
7. Biblical movie in the making, in wide screen. (7)
8. They're too often inflated (4)
9. ___ one's laurels (6)
12. Long and narrow (6)
13. Changed coif (5)
17. Kind of warfare (8)
18. Driver's calculation (3)
19. Clearance (8)
23. Golden-___ (4)
25. Secretary of State (7)
27. Police command (6)
29. Beat keeper (7)
30. Non-coastal regions (7)

## Down

1. Warmed the bench, maybe (7)
2. Abbreviated cross words (4)
3. Put forth, as power or influence (5)
4. Start to melt (6)
5. Harbinger (4)
6. "Whoa there, buddy!" (9)
10. Photo (8)
11. Tropical fruit that is one of the flavors in Hawaiian Punch (6)
14. Manning with two Super Bowl wins (3)
15. Name related to Inga (4)
16. "Quo Vadis? "emperor (4)
18. "Better ___ ..." (3)
20. Speed skater and past "Dancing with the Sta champ Apolo Anton ___ (4)
21. One of the guys (4)
22. Caviar source (6)

# Virtues

1. egsryneiot    generosity

   _____

2. cgrea    grace

   _____

3. aesgruiosscn    graciousness

   _____

4. edtiagutr    gratitude

   _____

5. eulsnhpefsl    helpfulness

   _____

6. nhsyteo    honesty

   _____

7. ohorn    honor

   _____

8. iitmyuhl    humility

   _____

9. sekdnnis    kindness

   _____

10. salmidei    idealism

    _____

11. imtpartliyia    impartiality

    _____

12. uslsfnoejy    joyfulness

    _____

13. neinoncec    innocence

    _____

14. etiitgyrn    integrity

    _____

15. laytoly    loyalty

    _____

## Positive Words with 5 Letters

1. egera    agree

   _____

2. sibsl    bliss

   _____

3. vebar    brave

   _____

4. lncea    clean

   _____

5. hesrf    fresh

   _____

6. trega    great

   _____

7. lhuag    laugh

   _____

8. cluyk    lucky

   _____

9. qutei    quiet

   _____

10. hirtg    right

    _____

11. imles    smile

    _____

12. opudr    proud

    _____

13. vlita    vital

    _____

14. strtu    trust

    _____

15. loehw    whole

    _____

# Matching Duo
Find the match for each item

| | | |
|---|---|---|
| 1. | d | mom |
| 2. | h | divide |
| 3. | a | fire |
| 4. | k | rock |
| 5. | m | war |
| 6. | n | skull |
| 7. | i | death |
| 8. | g | question |
| 9. | b | stars |
| 10. | l | motherhood |
| 11. | j | flotsam |
| 12. | e | ebony |
| 13. | f | xylem |
| 14. | c | mad dogs |

a. brimstone
b. stripes
c. Englishman
d. pop
e. ivory
f. phloem
g. answer
h. conquer
i. taxes
j. jetsam
k. hard place
l. apple pie
m. peace
n. bones

# Opposites
Write the letter of the correct matching opposite word next to each problem.

| | | |
|---|---|---|
| 1. | h | brave |
| 2. | g | build |
| 3. | k | bold |
| 4. | a | borrow |
| 5. | i | diseased |
| 6. | b | down |
| 7. | c | downwards |
| 8. | f | dreary |
| 9. | d | dry |
| 10. | e | minority |
| 11. | j | intentional |
| 12. | l | humble |

a. lend
b. up
c. upwards
d. moist
e. majority
f. cheerful
g. destroy
h. cowardly
i. healthy
j. accidental
k. meek
l. proud

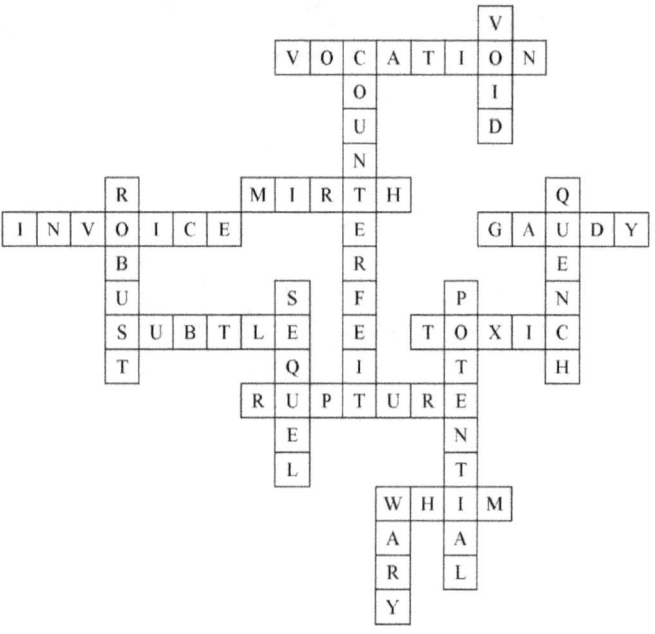

- VOID
- WARY
- WHIM
- GAUDY
- MIRTH
- TOXIC
- QUENCH
- ROBUST
- SEQUEL
- SUBTLE
- INVOICE
- RUPTURE
- VOCATION
- POTENTIAL
- COUNTERFEIT

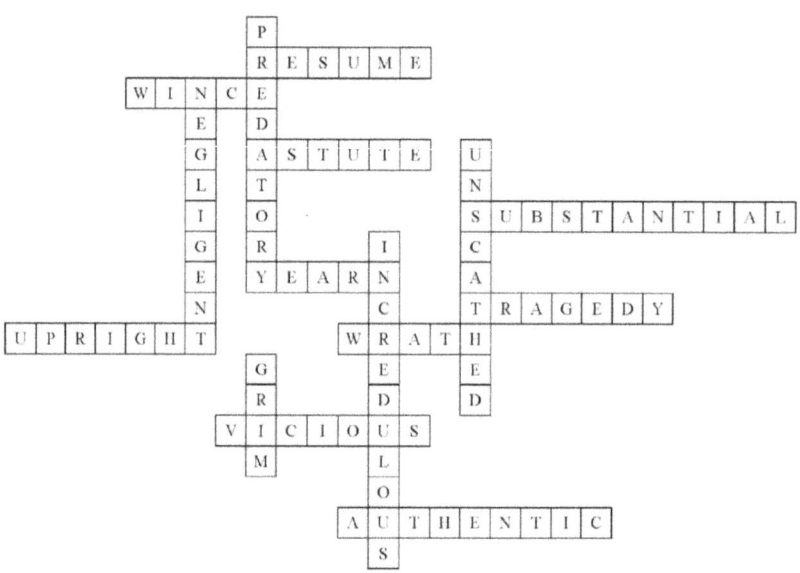

- GRIM
- WINCE
- WRATH
- YEARN
- ASTUTE
- RESUME
- TRAGEDY
- UPRIGHT
- VICIOUS
- AUTHENTIC
- NEGLIGENT
- PREDATORY
- UNSCATHED
- INCREDULOUS
- SUBSTANTIAL

# Mazes

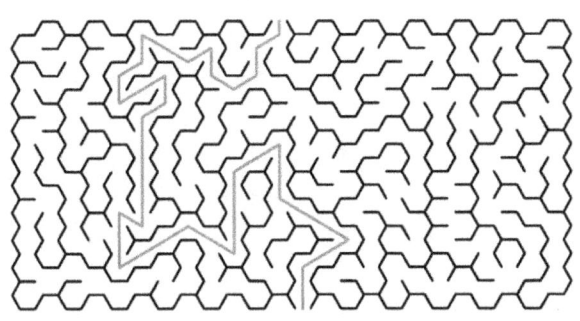

# Word Search

## Puzzle 1

```
K V F U N D A M E N T A L L A C I S U M
D R W W Z E T Q P C P U U C W E A P O N
O G H L U A O T R E E C L X U P P C N I
C M E E O T G R A E F O L M V C K E M H
U Y I B D O K I S S T O Z G A T H E R I
M L M S E X U A L H W C H R O A D S Y H
E E A P P R O X I M A T E L Y B Y S W W
N R V S C F L N D I N I N G S T L A B H
T D R K U E G B C G N I D D E W R L C X
L E A A G O O E U U O Q R E O A G E E E
V F P A E B R I G B O J O V C S E A E G
O I L I D N N E S D I Y A M D G U R C B
C C U L A S G E G A E C Q D Z Y F B I Q
G I W H T N R Q H N T L E V O B A D D J
E T G A E V O F R I A B W S W O U C B R
K M N O A A I O V Q C D U O D T P B D E
X C E T G G V I S O R R Y E N D Q U R V
E P I H H H S G A L E N A P I K O W C I
Q O S T C T U D O C T O R Y C L C K J X
N M W A X S H T R O W N N I C Q U A N W
```

## Puzzle 2

```
J X I N T E L L E C T U A L C S L L E W
F U B H G Q B N E D I S A P P E A R N F
M B T E B E W C C W M S I N A H C E M R
N W U D L C C N T C A R T N O C Q E E R
E K M J S O M I A V E R O U G H L Y X Q
R I X D W D N H T E N T I R E L Y R P U
K A O N C K K G S O I P R O C E E D E E
X M E V F P W L I W N M E T I V N I N I
J C B G C F U A S M O V I X T U W F S O
O Q R P X M T T A D A K S J K L K V G Y
N E O U T R I A F I R Y U P S Y P N I V
E P M F I W M C T T M Y N F V S I S U M
W R I Q M N B K A O E Q P Z Z W O Z M U
O E N Z D R U P S R D K P R A Q A R T Z
L T E E A L S B Z U V Z Y R E W R Q C Z
L E N T T S E R R A H E D E I U P Y D O
O N T V N G B N X O L A U T I R I P S F
F D H I G H L Y R A N M C A P A B L E B
T O O L Z Q V D Z A H D E C I S I O N X
```

## Puzzle 3

```
C F O U N D A T I O N M R O T A C U D E
O U N V O C H E D L L A R E V O M E V I
N A A E U H G E N B P M I E E P A C S E
S S S E U G I T B X O A K E T Y M T K Z V
E N G C F L I A O E L U N A B L E G P E
N O Y O D D N T X A Z M S J B I K A
S H R M B H S H Q A P P R E C I A T E U
U E E M C O T R K O S B Y B L A I C O S
S E V A T O R O E Q Y L L A I C E P S E
O D O N E D U O B R E C O M M E N D P G
T I C D R X C M I W A D N E G A E Q Q E
O H S C M H T C Y M E T A R E P S E D N
W E I H S F I O T E C S C O V F E O T E
A U D A E F O F I L T P L O T S W B X R
R S R T J Y N F R E S R E S E M B L E A
D D Q B T D Z E B C R O V R L O M R P T
S L C H A R G E E T I Y T C I Q J W A I
M O I L J N M V L X F E Q X O T O E E O
P C K N A T T V E J P I O C E A A N H N
T A G N O S H I C F D G G R B N F K C X
```

# Word Search

## Puzzle 4

## Puzzle 5

## Puzzle 6

# Odd One Out

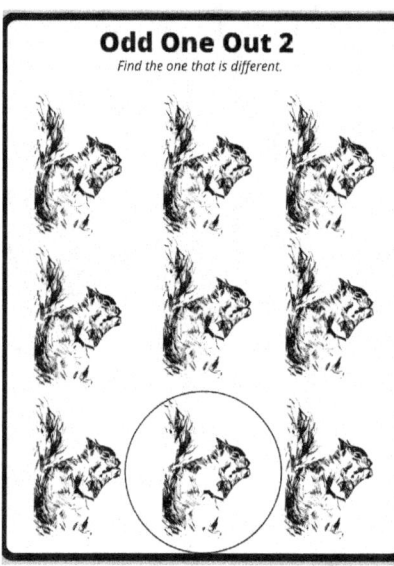

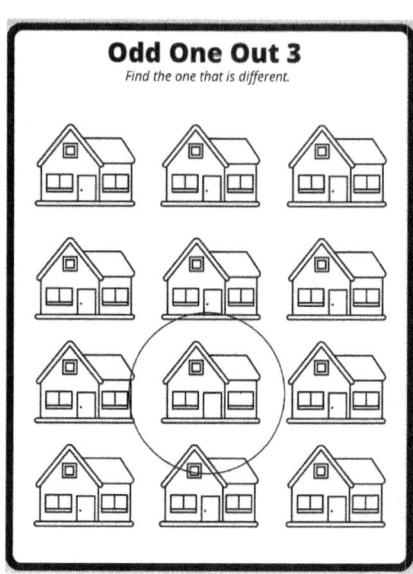

# Slice puzzles

## Puzzle 1

## Puzzle 2

## Puzzle 3

# Kakuro

## Puzzle 1

## Puzzle 2

## Puzzle 3

Thank you for purchasing this book! Do you enjoy Would You Rather questions? We want you to keep having fun, so as a special thank you please download this FREE gift:

# 201 Would You Rather questions!

The questions come in a pdf that you can download to your phone and easily take with you on your next trip to enjoy with your family and friends!

# Download here:

https://linktr.ee/mattisonsavage

If you enjoyed this book please consider leaving a review online. Your feedback helps us make more and better books for you.

# Thank you!